W0232441

HEALTHY
HABITS FOR
TEACHER LIFE

HEALTHY HABITS FOR TEACHER LIFE

{ Charlie Burley }

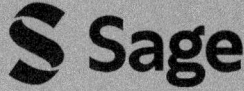

1 Oliver's Yard
55 City Road
London EC1Y 1SP

2455 Teller Road
Thousand Oaks
California 91320

Unit No 323-333, Third Floor, F-Block
International Trade Tower
Nehru Place, New Delhi – 110 019

8 Marina View Suite 43-053
Asia Square Tower 1
Singapore 018960

Editor: Amy Thornton
Senior project editor: Chris Marke
Cover design: Wendy Scott
Typeset by: C&M Digitals (P) Ltd, Chennai, India
Printed by CPI Group (UK) Ltd, Croydon CR0 4YY

**Library of Congress Control Number:
2024951339**

**British Library Cataloguing in
Publication data**

A catalogue record for this book is available from the British Library

ISBN 978-1-0362-0108-1(pbk)

This book is dedicated to *you*.

Our teachers, support staff, leaders, administration staff, SENCOs, midday assistants, site managers and everyone else involved in helping nurture our next generation.

Thank you will never be enough.

ACKNOWLEDGEMENTS

I'd like to briefly thank some of the awesome humans who have helped bring this book to life.

Firstly, thank you to Amy and Sage Publications for giving me this incredible opportunity, and for your patience and understanding during the process.

A special thank you to my good friend Johnny Lawrence – the self-development coach, not the guy from *Karate Kid*! I'll be forever grateful to you for your unwavering support, empathy, friendship and belief. From the bottom of my heart, thank you mate.

I need to mention my amazing clients, you know who you are. I wouldn't be the coach I am today without your trust and support. I can't thank you enough and I'm forever grateful for you. This is *our* book.

My friends, especially Amy, Mike and Chris. Thank you for looking out for me, for your endless patience with me and always believing in, and supporting, everything I do.

I'd also like to thank the online teacher community, especially over on Instagram. Thank you for your support of everything I do and everything we're trying to achieve. You are amazing. This book happened because of *you*.

And, finally, most importantly, my incredible fiancée, Sharna. You're my partner in every sense of the word. Thank you for all your love, support and blind belief in me. I wouldn't be here without you.

There are so many people I need to thank and not enough space. I'll send you a copy instead.

TABLE OF CONTENTS

{ ABOUT THIS BOOK }

Empowering teachers to live their healthiest, happiest lives and to thrive both in and out of the classroom, this practical, realistic guide for teachers, supports them to develop and maintain the behaviours, beliefs and boundaries they need for a positive teacher life.

- Authored by experts in the field
- Easy to dip in and out of
- Interactive activities encourage you to write into the book and make it your own
- Fun, engaging illustrations throughout
- Read in an afternoon or take as long as you like with it

Find out more at
www.sagepub.co.uk/littleguides

ABOUT THE SERIES

A LITTLE GUIDE FOR TEACHERS series is little in size but big on all the support and inspiration you need to navigate your day-to-day life as a teacher.

 CASE STUDY

 HINTS & TIPS

 REFLECTION

 RESOURCES

 NOTE THIS DOWN

ABOUT THE AUTHOR

Charlie Burley is a former primary school teacher turned nutritionist, coach, speaker and author. Director of the Teachers' Health Coach Ltd, Charlie focuses on helping teachers and school staff live their healthiest, happiest lives by building bitesize behaviours for their wellbeing. After five years in the classroom, he experienced burnout and was later diagnosed with chronic stress and anxiety. Charlie subsequently undertook his own journey of recovery and discovery that helped him to return to the classroom, and took him into a career in health coaching. He has a hands-on understanding of the challenges his clients, the *teachers' team*, face on a daily basis through both personal experience and the experience of coaching over a thousand teachers, leaders and school staff with their wellbeing. Grounded in neuroscience, psychology and coaching, Charlie's work focuses on helping teachers build healthier habits, manage their mental health and create mindset shifts so they can finally thrive, both in and out of the classroom. Whether it's directly with private clients, through his work in schools across the UK, or his *Rewriting Wellbeing* events, Charlie is passionate about empowering educators to make realistic, manageable change with their wellbeing that lasts a lifetime.

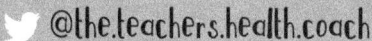 @the.teachers.health.coach

INTRODUCTION

I'm about to discuss the topic of anxiety and give a description of my experience of a panic attack. In case these topics are triggering for you, I wanted to let you know.

In early May 2019, after five years in teaching, I was standing in front of my Year 6 class when I had what I can only describe as one of the most frightening experiences of my life.

The children were coming back into the classroom after breaktime. A child, who found it challenging to regulate their emotions, was finding things very difficult after an incident during football at breaktime. They came flying into the classroom, hands aloft and voice very much raised. It wasn't long before pencils, books and a few chairs were flying across the classroom.

Suddenly, it hit me.

The rapid and heavy heartbeat, the inability to control my breathing and the sense of dread crashed down on me like a tidal wave. It felt like someone had tipped a fridge over on my chest. At that moment, I was convinced I was having a heart attack and nothing you could have said would have made me think otherwise. The room was closing in and I just had to get out. It was only the second time I had experienced a panic attack. Since that day I've experienced many more. But, why? This wasn't a particularly challenging incident for me at this stage in my career, surely?

At the time, I was still processing the end of a five-year relationship. My lovely learning support assistant, Sally, who had quickly become something of a grandmother figure to me in the time we'd worked together, had been losing her battle with cancer and would very soon pass away. It was also a week or two before the 2019 end of Key Stage 2 SATs. I hadn't realised how much these events, and the day-to-day toll of teaching, had affected me until it was too late.

To cut a long story short, I was subsequently sent home, visited by a paramedic and then spent a day in hospital being poked and prodded. The conclusion?

Chronic stress and anxiety.

So why am I sharing this with you? There are a few reasons really, but mostly it's to show that I can genuinely understand how bad things can get if we don't make time for our health – mental or physical. Also, I wanted to be totally honest about the fact that I didn't have many of these habits ingrained before I burnt out, but successfully put them in place during my recovery and beyond; hopefully this shows that these habits *can* be developed while being a full-time teacher and, in many cases, a parent, carer or guardian too.

> *IF you don't make time For your wellness,*
> *You'll be Forced to take time For your illness.*
> Anon

As you might have guessed, the story doesn't end there. Following this, I went on a six-month journey of recovery and discovery, leading me to be able to get back in the classroom. I experienced the best years of my career, personally and professionally, and decided to formally qualify as a nutritionist, coach and mental health and exercise coach. Over the last five years, I've researched, designed and refined the strategies I'm about to share with you to help over a thousand tired, time-short teachers transform their health and wellbeing and, finally, thrive – both in and out the classroom.

Before we wrap up this quick introduction, I just want to take a moment to acknowledge *you*. By purchasing this book (thank you, by the way), you have taken a much bigger step than you might realise. Every choice we make in life compounds to build our self-image and, by starting this book, you have made the choice to build your identity as someone who values, prioritises and lives a healthy, happy life. That's pretty awesome.

There's so much I wanted to include in this book and just not enough space, so I've kept each chapter extremely practical and to the point. I've included some resources and further reading at the back to help build on what we'll cover. However, if you would like to discuss anything in detail, please feel free to drop me an email at charlie@theteachershealthcoach.co.uk or message me on any of my social media platforms. I'll be happy to help.

Let's get stuck in ...

CHAPTER 1
HOW CAN I BUILD HEALTHY HABITS THAT LAST?

This chapter explores the following ideas:

- small steps compound to create lasting change and manageable actions are crucial to set yourself up for success
- how environment is the key to building healthy habits and how shaping your space supports your goals
- having a backup plan is a must to help you keep consistent.

UNDERSTANDING 'HABITS'

*First we form our habits, then they form us. Conquer
[your] habits, or they'll eventually conquer you.*
Dr Rob Gilbert, 2013

 ## REFLECTION 1.1

What habits do you want to build most right now? Why?

Habit hacking has become a hot topic in the health space in recent years. From the lockdown lifestyles most of us lived back in 2020 to the publication of incredibly successful books on behaviour, like *Atomic Habits* by James Clear, habit building has seen increased publicity across the media of late. Together these things have brought the topic to the attention of the masses.

This is good news for our health as teachers. After all, our life is just a series of small things we do daily, which eventually become our habits.

 ## REFLECTION 1.2

It might sound a bit too deep for the first five minutes of a book, but try to think ahead to the end of your days. Imagine looking back on a life well lived; a life you're truly proud of and content with. What will you have done? What will you have avoided? And, most importantly, what habits need to be a part of your day-to-day life to get there?

If we can learn about and design our habits, rather than letting them be decided by default, then we can reclaim control of our health – no matter how hectic things might get for us in school. Before we go any further, I think we need to define our terms. I've used several already: *habits, behaviours, actions* ... So what's the difference? Are they different? Habits are often misunderstood; they're commonly mixed up with behaviours – but there is a big difference.

DEFINING OUR TERMS

Behaviours (n): our individual actions, or reactions. Driven by many complex influences including psychological and physiological needs, conditioning, social norms, environment – even our genetics.

Habits (n): the 'automatic' and often unconscious patterns of behaviour formed through repetition and reinforcement which, through neuroplasticity, leads to structural changes in our brains.

Our habits are like subconscious systems in our brain which, despite being 'wired in', can be changed. Whereas behaviours happen due to the more discrete choices we make, or reactions we have.

HABITS YOU ARE NOT QUITE HAPPY WITH

 REFLECTION 1.3

What habits have you developed that you're not quite happy with? How would they affect your life if they were to continue for another 12 months?

It's important to try our best not to beat ourselves up for the habits we've built; many of them have developed from a need for psychological safety or soothing. Biting your nails, using food to regain control and even doom scrolling on social media all 'helped' us in some way initially. The difference is that what our brains think is best for us in the moment is rarely what we need to live our healthiest, happiest lives in the long run.

THE CONCEPT OF BITESIZE BEHAVIOURS

Have you ever set yourself a goal of building a healthy habit, managed to stick to it for a day or two and then completely fallen 'off the wagon' with it? *Yeah, me too!*

Habit building is complex. A 2009 study by Lally et al. found that it took 66 days on average for participants' actions to become automatic, but this is very much a ballpark figure. It actually took anywhere from 18 to 254 days. How long it takes depends on a variety of factors: number of repetitions, the scale of the habit, past experiences, neurodiversity, trauma, environment and many other influences. And this is just one study; others show that it can take up to a year.

Before we even think about habits, I want to focus on building what I call *bitesize behaviours*. Bitesize behaviours are the *minimal effective dose version* of the action you want to eventually build into a habit. Creating consistency with our health is hard enough as it is as teachers; we want to set ourselves up for success, not failure.

Here are some *big to bitesize* suggestions:

- going to the gym for an hour three times a week → three 15-minute home workouts

- not eating chocolate for a month → reducing it in your diet to a few times a week

- going to bed at 9pm rather than 12am → going upstairs 15 minutes earlier than usual.

 HINTS AND TIPS 1.1

Focusing on the smallest viable version of the action (the minimal effective dose), supports us to create consistency.

If we can establish consistency, we can move on to the fuels for our habits: *momentum* and *confidence*. Once we have that belief in ourselves, we can begin to increase the size or frequency of the behaviour.

 REFLECTION 1.4

Write down one to three bitesize behaviours you could begin implementing today that would take you one small step closer to that vision for your life we looked at earlier.

When considering these, ask yourself: is this *really* the minimal effective dose? Could I make this habit any more manageable for myself?

THE ROLE OF OUR ENVIRONMENTS

One sunny day, a young boy was walking down the pier with his father. As they walked, the boy spotted an elderly, weathered fisherman sitting on the edge with a silt-stained, broken bucket next to him. Subtly peering over the top of the bucket, the boy could see at least two dozen crabs of all shapes and sizes clambering over each other at the bottom.

As he watched, one crab clawed its way over the rest and made a daring dash for the top. The crab was mere millimetres away from getting out. 'Mr, Mr,' the boy exclaimed, 'your crabs are going to escape!'

Without looking up, the fisherman chuckled, 'Don't you worry, son. They ain't goin' nowhere.' As he spoke, the boy noticed the other crabs leaping and snipping for the renegade crustacean's legs and, as quickly as the crab climbed to the top, it was dragged back down.

The term 'crab mentality' is often used to explain how we behave in social groups: as a tribal species we like to see each other succeed, as long as it doesn't overshadow our success or highlight our insecurities. However, I think we can extend this metaphor more widely than just the people we surround ourselves with; I think it applies to our physical and mental environments too – the places we go and the perspectives we hold. When we're considering creating a new bitesize behaviour we have to set ourselves up for success with our environments. Our surroundings won't just provide (or hide) the cues we'll need to prompt us, they'll also make it easier (or harder) to actually take the action we're trying to. So it's important that our environments are created by design, not by default.

PHYSICAL SPACES

 REFLECTION 1.5

Consider your *physical spaces* for a second: your home, your car, your classroom or office. Right now, are they helping you or hindering you? What tiny tweaks could you make to help?

Visualise walking through your day: waking up, your morning routine, the breakfast you eat (if you eat one at all), travelling to work, all the way through to getting into bed later that evening. Focus on the physical elements of these routines. For example, if you're aiming to get out for a 15-minute morning walk but your trainers are at the back of the cupboard, it's going to be difficult; or if you're aiming to eat more fruit and fewer sweets but your car is full of sugar, this easy access might cause you some problems.

You might have noticed that there's a lot of friction between the physical space and some of those behaviours you're hoping will become habits. As teachers, life moves fast. We don't often take the time to pause and create space to think through how we're setting up our physical environments for success. Managing this is one of the simplest ways to improve our healthy habits.

Here are a few simple ideas:

- want to drink more water? Leave a full glass next to your bed

- want to stretch in the morning? Leave your yoga mat out on the floor

- want to walk more? Take the long way round to the photocopier

- want to stop scrolling? Start leaving your phone in a different room

- want to snack on fruit? Move the biscuit barrel out of sight and put the fruit bowl front and centre.

 HINTS AND TIPS 1.2

Complex, confusing systems only serve to keep us stuck in the on–off, stop–start cycle we've all experienced before.

Simplicity is the ultimate sophistication.
Leonardo da Vinci

SOCIAL ENVIRONMENTS

Next, let's think about your *social environments*. As humans we are a tribal species. Connection and safety with others are among our most inherent human needs. To truly thrive, we need our relationships to feel secure, safe and to support us. If you feel like you're being constantly gaslighted in school, overlooked for opportunities or simply unappreciated, it will be really challenging to build belief and confidence in yourself. This will directly impact your consistency with your healthy habits. Why would you bother putting effort into yourself if the message you're getting from others is that you're not worth it?

Of course, we can't always choose our colleagues and, as professionals, we do need to navigate the needs of others, routines and policies – and sometimes politics. However, if you feel someone is negatively impacting your health through how they're treating you then there are steps you can take:

- minimising contact and distancing yourself from that individual where possible

- trying to ensure the presence of another colleague when interacting with them

- contacting your union or organisation such as Education Support for advice

- following your workplace's policies to report their conduct

- or, the really uncomfortable one, having an honest and open conversation about how their actions are making you feel and setting out new expectations or boundaries – more on this in Chapter 2.

OUR MENTAL ENVIRONMENT

Finally, maybe the most complex space we exist in, our *mental environment*: the thoughts we have and the way we see ourselves and the world around us. As teachers, we may be very compassionate, caring and conscientious individuals. This is our greatest strength but can sometimes be our Achilles' heel too. It means we often attach our self-worth to our service to others and overdeliver from a place of insecurity. Limiting beliefs around setting boundaries, getting 'found out' or simply not being good enough can plague our self-talk causing us to feel guilty and leading us to deprioritise our needs as compared to the needs of others.

The truth is, our thoughts are not facts. This isn't to invalidate your thoughts or emotions, it's just the way it is. We each see the world through our own unique lens. Reality gives us the sketched outlines; we add the fine detail to the picture to make our own meaning. Just like our behaviours, they're influenced by so many internal and external factors. One quick strategy I like to use with clients is the idea of *thought court*. If you were to take this thought to court, would it hold up? What evidence is there? Would the jury hand out the sentence of true or false? This pragmatic approach can not only help us rationalise our thoughts, but also give us the opportunity to slow down and gain the perspective that we need.

 # REFLECTION 1.6

Visualise a day in the life of you, from beginning to end, the more detail the better. Think about the places, people and perspectives you come into contact with. Jot them down. For each, ask yourself if they're helping or hindering? Are they boosting you or draining you? Draw an up or down arrow next to each to show the impact.

BUILDING OUT YOUR RAPID ROUTINE ROADMAP

> *You do not rise to the level of your goals, you fall to the level of your systems.*
> James Clear, 2018

As teachers, we spend so much of our time meticulously timetabling and tweaking to make sure the children get everything they need in the small amount of time we have with them each day. We know how important small steps and systems are in order for us to get a child from A to B – be that emotionally, academically or socially. So how come we don't apply the same process to our healthy habits?

We've already discussed the importance of bitesize behaviours and the influence of environments on our habits, now let's get really practical and apply these concepts to create our own success system for our healthy habits using the *rapid routines roadmap*. Your roadmap will be a personalised series of steps that breaks down your actions into manageable chunks and ensures the routine, which will eventually become your habit, is really going to work.

As we do this, we can apply James Clear's Four Laws of Behaviour Change (2018) and the teachings of other experts in the field of habits and behaviour like B.J. Fogg and Charles Duhigg. Here are James Clear's Four Laws, alongside a brief summary:

- *make it obvious*: set clear cues, triggers and reminders
- *make it attractive*: it has to be enjoyable, especially at the start
- *make it easy*: start small and remove any friction
- *make it satisfying*: celebrate wins and reward yourself.

To help you build your roadmap, we're going to look at the 5Rs. These stages and questions will help you reflect on the most important aspects of building new behaviours and spot the barriers that might hinder you from building them successfully. The 5Rs are:

- *redesign*: what exactly is the behaviour I'm trying to build? *What* is the behaviour? *Who* is involved? *When* will it happen – before X, after Y? *Where* will it take place? *Why* is it important?
- *ready*: what can I physically prepare to reduce friction in performing the behaviour and create cues to act as my trigger? How can I make it more enjoyable?
- *rehearsal*: what will the behaviour look like when I complete it successfully? Mentally rehearse it in your mind
- *reward*: how will I reinforce the positive behaviour? How will I track it? How will I reward myself for completing a streak?

- *reflect*: periodically, ask what's gone well with the behaviour? How could it be even better?

Let's see how that might look for someone trying to build the habit of drinking a glass of water first thing in the morning before the rush of the day begins:

- *redesign*: I (*who*) will drink a large glass of lemon water (*what*) in bed (*where*) first thing in the morning, after I wake up and before I go to the toilet (*when*), so I can rehydrate to increase my energy levels and think more clearly in the morning (*why*)

- *ready*: I will take a full glass of lemon water up to bed with me each evening and will leave an empty glass in front of the kettle, ready to remind me again, in case I've already drunk it through the night

- *rehearsal*: I'll visualise a successful completion of the above, walking through the setup and execution of the behaviour – and the positive impacts

- *reward*: I will reinforce the behaviour by tracking these habits on a monthly calendar and ticking it off first thing after rehydrating. After a week, I'll buy myself a new bottle. After a month, I'll take myself out for a solo coffee date with a good book

- *reflect*: at the end of each week, I'll ask what's gone well with the behaviour? How could it be even better?

You can see that I've made the cues really obvious throughout the day: a glass next to my bed. I've also stacked the new behaviour onto an existing one – waking up. I've made it more enjoyable by buying myself a new water bottle and filling my glass with lemon. Finally, I've ended the habit by tracking it.

BUT, TEACHER LIFE? PREPARING FOR ALL EVENTUALITIES

Let's be honest, even the best laid plans often go awry as a teacher. We can't expect ourselves to be perfect with our healthy habits. In fact, aiming for perfection often keeps us stuck as we suffer with 'paralysis by analysis' and feel like we've failed, even when we've made great progress. We need to be realistic and accept that sometimes things won't go to plan and give ourselves the same compassion and kindness we show to others on a daily basis.

This is where the concept of *ABC planning* comes in. In school, we always have a Plan B. We know how to adapt lessons, shift around our day or provide a positive experience for the children even in the worst situations; a child having a *very* poorly tummy in the middle of a Year 1 gymnastics lesson, during my final placement observation with my university tutor comes to mind ...

 HINTS AND TIPS 1.3

Think *frequency not intensity*. To build habits, we need to build and strengthen neural pathways through the process of neuroplasticity; it's more about the repetitions than the scale of the behaviour. If you have the aim of becoming a 6am runner, you would be better off running for five minutes most mornings at 6am than once a week for 35 minutes on a Saturday.

ABC PLANNING

ABC planning is the concept of creating three tiers of your behaviours to take the pressure off and create consistency:

- *A-game*: you're flying high, operating at 80 per cent or more. Energy is high, stress is moderate and your fuse is long. This is when we can increase our expectations. Maybe we aim to get an extra workout in, get ahead with our planning or prep a few days' worth of meals. This is the time to challenge your limits and be your future friend for those darker days.

- *Plan B*: things are starting to get a bit tough – you've probably spent a lot of your time as a teacher here. Maybe you're functioning at about 60 per cent. Energy is a little lower, patience is minimal and your risk of becoming overwhelmed is real. This is where we pull back a bit. We'd like to still keep most of our actions, but maybe we reduce them slightly. That gym session you planned might become a 15-minute home workout; finishing your to-do list might become ticking off only the few most urgent tasks; journalling through your day may be best swapped for writing down just one thing that went well.

- *C–risis point:* okay, so now you're working with only 20 per cent or so. You haven't slept well, you're dragging yourself through the day, absolutely everything feels like a chore. Now is not the time to set your sights high; let's reduce our expectations and focus on simply nourishing and recovering. This is when the Five Foundations become our baseline.

 # REFLECTION 1.7

Map out your own ABC approach for one to three core habits that you're trying to build. What do the three tiers look like for you?

THE FIVE FOUNDATIONS

The Five Foundations is one of the very first systems I created back when I first began coaching friends, family and colleagues. To this day, it's remained one of the most impactful ideas I introduce clients to. These basics form the base for our mental and physical health and give us impactful but achievable actions we can take. They are, each day:

- get 6-8 hours' sleep
- drink 1.5-3 litres of water

- walk 8–10,000 steps

- eat 4–6 portions of fruit and vegetables

- take 15–30 minutes for you.

Auditing these areas is always my starting point with any teacher I coach. You'll notice that the foundations are ranged. This is because everyone's needs and starting points are different, so it's difficult to put a definite number on it. Simply start from where you are right now and, using the concept of the minimal effective dose, gradually build upon your starting point until you're within these ranges. If you're someone who doesn't like attaching numbers to things, feel free to go by feel; the idea behind the foundations is still the same: focus on the small, daily basics and build up slowly.

 # REFLECTION 1.8

Spend some time reflecting on the Five Foundations. With 0 being low and 10 being high, how would you rate these healthy behaviours in your life at the moment? Which ones need the most attention? Why?

NOTE IT DOWN

WE'RE GOING TO BUILD YOUR OWN RAPID ROUTINE ROADMAP FOR ONE SMALL BEHAVIOUR YOU'D LIKE TO BEGIN BUILDING THIS WEEK.

REMEMBER, FOCUS ON THE MINIMAL EFFECTIVE DOSE. OUR BRAINS WILL TEND TO ENCOURAGE US TO TAKE THE MOST 'EFFECTIVE' ACTION. THIS WILL LIKELY MEAN THAT WE LEAN TOWARDS GOING FROM 0-100 OVERNIGHT, WHICH FEELS IMPACTFUL BUT IS OFTEN UNSUSTAINABLE. REDUCE YOUR EXPECTATIONS AND BE KIND TO YOURSELF AS YOU PLAN OUT YOUR NEW BEHAVIOURS.

REDESIGN:

READY:

REHEARSAL:

REWARD:

REFLECT:

CHAPTER 2
HOW CAN I CREATE SPACE FOR MY HEALTH?

This chapter explores the following ideas:

- establishing boundaries protects your wellbeing and can't be avoided, even if it means saying no or risking disappointing others
- clarity and confidence are key to building boundaries; this comes from clearly defining them, communicating them and maintaining them consistently
- boundaries create a positive ripple effect and have a powerful impact on those around you, reinforcing the value of wellbeing for all.

UNDERSTANDING 'HABITS'

It can be tempting, in our goal-oriented society, to push ourselves beyond our capacities in pursuit of success. But when we do this we tell ourselves that our work is more important than our health. Without our health our success means nothing. No promotion, no raise. No accolade will mean anything if you aren't happy and healthy.
Olivia Kram, 2021

ESTABLISHING BOUNDARIES

Although this book isn't focused on workplace wellbeing, workload or productivity, we can't talk about teachers' health without at least briefly touching on these topics. So let's begin by looking at boundaries, at how we can make setting out your stall more manageable. There are a few that are key for us as teachers:

- *emotional* boundaries – your emotions: separating your own while supporting others'

- *moral* boundaries – your ethics: beliefs, integrity, moral guidelines

- *intellectual* boundaries – your professional expertise: opinions, ideas, perspectives, skills

- *time* boundaries – your time: managing meetings, contracted hours, additional responsibilities

- *material* boundaries – in short, your stuff: gluesticks, resources, coffee granules

- *social* boundaries – your interactions: conversations, social commitments, time with colleagues.

 # REFLECTION 2.1

Which boundaries do you currently hold fast and feel most confident with?

Which areas do you feel need redesigning and reaffirming?

Boundaries can't be fixed. Especially working in education, they'll need to ebb and flow at times; that's okay. Like with our health, it's important to focus on the patterns over time. Are people constantly overstepping in a certain area? Are you gradually teaching people to expect a certain behaviour from you somewhere? Our boundaries need to bend sometimes, but it's important that we don't allow them to break altogether.

THE 3CS OF BUILDING BETTER BOUNDARIES

Like with anything, until we have awareness around an issue it's almost impossible to effectively address it. In order for us to build better boundaries, and communicate them well so that others understand them, we need to get crystal clear on our own expectations first. I've simplified the process down in three simple steps:

- *clarity*: *what* actually is the boundary? *Who* is involved? *When* and *where* will it take place, if applicable? What does it look like for you (and others)? What might challenge the boundary? *Why* is it important for you to set it?

- *communication*: this is how you actually set the boundary. It's important you explain it clearly, state the consequence of it not being followed (for others and for yourself) and get confirmation from everyone involved that it's understood

- *checking in*: unfortunately, setting boundaries isn't a one-time deal. Like a garden, you have to maintain them, water them and sometimes get the weed killer out. Reinforcing boundaries is uncomfortable, but it's necessary.

HINTS AND TIPS 2.1

There's no need to apologise or ask permission when setting a boundary.

We often start with an apology, infusing these conversations with lots of our own emotions. For example: *'This is really difficult. Erm ... I'm really sorry. But, erm ... Can I ...?'* and absorbing blame where we don't need to. You can absolutely thank the person(s) for their understanding, but you don't need to apologise for protecting your own health; in fact, you might just be giving others the confidence to do the same.

> *Daring to set boundaries is about having the courage to love ourselves even when we risk disappointing others.*
> Brené Brown, 2018

SCRIPTS FOR SAYING NO

As we've already established, saying no can be one of the most difficult things for us to do in school, but there *is* a time and a place for it. I'm a big believer in the fact that we teach people how to treat us. It's far too easy for us to become the *yes person* when we want to do well – and be seen doing well too. So, I've prepared some simple scripts you might want to use when reaffirming some of those boundaries.

- 'Thank you so much for thinking of me, I really appreciate that. I can't help at the moment but can you keep me in mind for future opportunities?'

- 'I'd love to help but I've been asked to work on *project name*. I don't want to rush and do half a job with it; can it wait until I've finished?'

- 'I'm afraid I don't work after _time_ on _day of the week_. Can we discuss this when we're both working in school tomorrow? Thanks.'

- 'Thanks for your email and for keeping me in the loop, I really appreciate that. It all sounds great but at the moment I don't have any room in my workload. I'll be able to help you after _date_; does that work for you?'

- 'I don't think I'm the best person to help you with this as _reason for declining_. Would it be possible to ask someone else to lead this instead?'

- 'I'm happy to do this but I've been asked to do _project name_ in this _timeframe_. Would you like me to make this my priority and put _project name_ on hold?'

- 'I'm afraid I've already committed to _project name_ and that needs to come first at the moment. Is there another way we could do this?'

Note how these ideas are clear, professional and polite, but hold boundaries firm and don't apologise or absorb blame from the situation.

REWIRING TO THE RIPPLE EFFECT

Our beliefs about ourselves and the world are built on evidence – real or perceived. The only real way to shift our perspectives around putting ourselves first is to provide our brain with the evidence that shows that, when we are a priority, _everyone wins_. Maybe not instantly, but over time; what's best for us will become best for the group. We need to show our minds that it's not _me or them_ and it's certainly not _selfish,_ it's _self-first_. We have to identify the positive ripples that happen as a result.

Let's take the example of a class teacher and explore just one ripple they could create. This person positively impacts the lives of the 30 children they teach; those 30 children go home to, on average, households with three to four family members; those family members go and interact with another 30 individuals at school or work and so on and so forth. Using just this example, by putting yourself first and showing up as your best self, you could easily positively impact the lives of 2,700 members of the local community!

HINTS AND TIPS 2.2

Never underestimate the powerful impact that looking after your health can have on those around you.

CREATING CONFIDENCE WITH BOUNDARIES

But how? How can I rewire my mindset to feel more confident with drawing boundaries and putting myself first?

I call this the *confidence creator*. It actually works with any area we might be doubting ourselves in, but for now let's focus on prioritising our health. For this to work we need to take just a couple of minutes most days to review the new evidence we've gathered; try tagging this onto an existing habit to make it easier to remember – before bed, for example. It works like this: we simply write out the new action we've taken and next to it write the positive impact it's had.

REFLECTION 2.2

Think about an action you have taken that has had a positive impact. Take time to really think about the ripple effect of that action.

By regularly repeating this process we begin to build the collection of evidence we need to reframe our perspectives. You can also do this more generally by saving positive feedback, screenshotting comments or keeping note of compliments people have paid you: it works wonders as long as you regularly revisit it.

PROTECTING YOUR PEACE

At the time of writing this book, life has never moved faster – especially life in school. We've also never been as distracted as we are today; we have notifications on all our devices, numerous tabs open at any given time and the content we consume on social media is often less than ten seconds long. This rapid acceleration of our world has done nothing for our attention and focus. So I want to give you some quick tips for helping you protect your attention, firewall your focus and increase your productivity as a byproduct.

- *The Pareto Principle*: 20 per cent of your tasks will give you 80 per cent of the results you want. Find the 20 per cent and focus your time there; it'll pay back dividends.

- *Focus music*: binaural beats, soundscapes and classical music have all been shown to increase focus and minimise distractions.

- *The Pomodoro Technique*: in its most basic form, work for 25 or 55 minutes and take a 5- or 15-minute break respectively. Focused work followed by allowing the brain to rest and wander.

- *Do one thing*: in their book, *The ONE Thing* (2013), Gary Keller and Jay Papasan talk about focusing on only the single most important task to maximise your chances of success.

- *Human aeroplane mode*: this one often makes my clients laugh, but cut out all distractions. Turn off the phone, or at least the notifications, put on music, put your earphones in, put a sign on the door, go home – do whatever you need to do to avoid distraction and increase your focus.

- *Properly prioritise*: there are many formats – the *must, should, could columns,* the *Eisenhower Matrix (4Ds)* or simply only allowing *three priorities* on your to-do list. To paraphrase Jim Collins in his book *Good to Great* (2001), if you've got more than three priorities, you haven't got priorities – you've got another list!

NOTE IT DOWN

Think about the boundary you feel is the most important for your mental and physical health right now. Look back at the section 'The 3Cs of building better boundaries' in this chapter. How would the 3Cs sound for this boundary?

CLARITY:

COMMUNICATION:

CHECKING IN:

CHAPTER 3
HOW CAN I MANAGE MY MENTAL HEALTH TO FEEL MY BEST?

This chapter explores the ideas that:

- there are many influences on our mental health as we work in education; understanding this is essential to managing our mental health
- focusing on the small, practical steps we can take each day that empower us rather than overwhelm us is key
- not all 'self-care' is created equal; sometimes we have to focus on the more effortful actions rather than the 'nice to dos' to effectively support our health.

IMPORTANT NOTE

In this chapter I will be discussing mental *health* not mental *illness* and it's incredibly important that we define them both and differentiate between the two. The definitions of these two terms vary widely, even within the NHS. I've consolidated several in a way that I hope gives a comprehensive overview.

- *Mental health* is the state of our emotional, psychological and social wellbeing that influences how we think, feel and act. It shapes our resilience to stress, the quality of our relationships and our capacity to meaningfully engage in life.

- *Mental illness* refers to a range of conditions, sometimes called disorders, that affect a person's mood, thinking and behaviour, often causing distress that impacts daily life, relationships and overall functioning. It includes disorders like anxiety, depression and schizophrenia.

We all have mental health, just as we all have physical health, but we will not all experience a mental illness or a mental disorder.

THE WEATHER OF YOUR MIND

When it comes to tackling low mood, we have to focus on making good decisions, not perfect decisions. A good decision is one that moves you in the direction you want to go. It doesn't have to catapult you there.
Dr Julie Smith, 2022

As we touched on above, definitions and terms around mental health and wellbeing can be complicated and change depending on where you look and who you talk to; I think it's important for each of us to define our own terms and build our own understanding of what mental health means to us. I like to use the weather as an analogy.

THE WEATHER (MOOD)

Just like the weather, our mood can be fickle. We can wake up after a great night's sleep and feel positive, resilient and motivated. But something as small as spilling our coffee or running out of petrol on the way to work can cause the clouds to come out and cover the sunshine – almost instantly, too. Like the weather, our mood can change quickly and is often impacted by external factors. How you feel in one moment doesn't need to be how you feel forever.

THE CLIMATE (MENTAL HEALTH)

Our mental health is a little bit like those weather patterns over time, or the 'climate' we're currently in. Although it may feel fixed year to year, or even decade to decade, just like the climate, our mental health can change too – positively and negatively. This fact that our mental health is malleable and we can make a real difference to how we feel over time is, again like the climate, something that's often ignored.

FACTORS THAT INFLUENCE OUR MENTAL HEALTH

As someone who works in a school, it's estimated that you make somewhere between 1,500 and 3,000 decisions during the day – and that's just while the children are there! That's roughly a decision every seven to 12 seconds. Personally, I think it's probably a lot higher than that given the hyper-vigilance we experience as educators. Not only are we making decisions about the children, but we're also deciding what we need to be doing at any given time.

But that's just the beginning. I've found that there are typically five reasons we often feel stressed and mentally fatigued as those working in education.

1. CHRONIC CORTISOL

Teaching is a full-on job; we're always 'on' and often required to be hyper-vigilant. Our bodies respond to this prolonged stress by releasing a cocktail of chemicals which include adrenaline, noradrenaline and cortisol (the stress hormones) priming our bodies for survival amid the threat we're facing. In the short term, this isn't a problem; cortisol does its job, we deal with the stressor and our bodies regulate themselves. But in teaching, the stressors often don't go away.

Chronic cortisol buildup can lead to a constant state of alertness, draining out energy reserves and stopping us from being able to switch off and relax. If we don't manage this response, we can experience insomnia, a loss of libido, weight gain or loss, fluctuations in appetite, hair loss and many other negative physical and psychological effects.

2. THOUGHT FATIGUE

You know that thick fog of overwhelm? You can't think clearly about even the simplest decisions. *'Do you want pizza or pasta for dinner?'* It feels like you're being asked to decide the fate of the Earth. Decision-making, problem-solving and constant multitasking are the bread and butter of what we do as teachers. You've heard the statistic about us making more minute-by-minute decisions than a brain surgeon, right? But the truth is, our brains can't actually multitask – they can only *task switch*.

The term 'multitasking' was coined in the 1960s and referred to computers performing more than one task a time – something they're still not great at, by the way. Our brains aren't brilliant at this either. Instead, they actually task switch very quickly between things we're placing our focus on. This continuous cognitive load results in thought fatigue. Our mental processes end up slowing down, making even smaller jobs and decisions feel extremely overwhelming.

3. PERPETUAL PATIENCE

Managing a classroom, a department or even a school requires seemingly endless amounts of patience. Unfortunately, that's the one resource we can't create. Although it seems simple, patience is actually a really complex trait and it uses multiple parts of the brain: the prefrontal cortex, the amygdala, the striatum and others. Plus, it relies on important chemicals in the brain like dopamine and serotonin … I'm getting tired just thinking about it.

Whether it's challenging behaviour, supporting struggling children or navigating the never-ending expectations of parents, the need to remain calm and composed is exhausting. This perpetual need for patience chips away at our mental energy and emotional resilience.

4. TRICKLE-DOWN TRAUMA

We often absorb the emotions in our environment – something we know all too well as those working in education. Seeing the children's challenges, struggles and, quite frankly, sometimes upsetting circumstances can take a significant toll on our own mental health as we ruminate on the situation. *Secondary trauma stress* is closely linked to PTSD and can leave us with intrusive thoughts, emotional numbness and heightened anxiety. This trickle-down trauma adds another layer to our emotional exhaustion.

5. EMOTIONAL EXHAUSTION

Teaching is a profession built on relationships, but this also means the emotional investment we put into our children's success and wellbeing is enormous. Over time, this deep emotional engagement can leave us feeling depleted and detached from our own emotions, and the emotions of others.

Sadly, so many of the conditions we face every day as teachers (the lack of control, last-minute changes, insufficient rest and emotional recovery) exaggerate these symptoms and make recovery even more challenging.

So, the important question: what can we do about it?

 REFLECTION 3.1

Think about these five areas for a moment. Can you think of examples from your own life? Which of these feels most true to you? Can you link any back to experiences you've had recently?

(Continued)

This reflection is simply about noticing. When we're trying to create any change, there are four stages we must go through: awareness, acceptance, accountability and action. Here we're not blaming or trying to change, we're simply noticing and building awareness around some of those events we experience day to day.

ADDRESSING STRESS: YOUR CAPACITY CUP

The *stress bucket* is a well-worn analogy that you've probably heard before. It's the idea that all our stress flows into one bucket, be it mental, physical or emotional. For example, if you're training hard in the gym, it places a stress on your central nervous system. Likewise, if you are facing a frustrated parent who raises their voice and you feel threatened, this too is a stress on the mind and body.

With my clients, I like to talk about the *capacity cup*. This is a similar idea, but focuses more on the *ownership* and *practical action* you can take to help manage your mental load – which, as you know by now, is what I'm all about.

Imagine for a moment a small paper cup. You know, one of those flimsy, awkwardly angled cone cups that holds about three drops of water and doesn't stand up on its own. This is us when we're feeling tired, busy-brained and less-than-resilient. As the stressors (the water) flow in, it doesn't take much for us to feel overwhelmed and for the stress to overflow all over our shoes – this is you reaching crisis point.

There are three main ways we can improve our capacity cup.

1. Step one is to change the cup's shape and material, and to increase its size. These are your *proactive strategies* – the things you can do that help you feel more calm, collected and in control. These could be things like planning out your day, taking 15 minutes in the morning for you, charging your phone away from your bed, getting to sleep sooner, etc. These are the things you can do ahead of stress starting. Once you've got these basic strategies in place your cup is solid, made of thicker material and – most importantly – has a flat bottom!

2. Now our cup is solid and we've increased our resilience and capacity for stress, we can start to think about ways to stop some of the stress coming in – like placing a lid on your cup. Sure, there might be a few holes in the lid, but it's much better than having no lid at all. These are those *boundaries* we covered in the last chapter. Pop back and reread the 3Cs framework if you need to.

3. And, to round off our capacity cup analogy, we need to look at how we can manage the stress that does still flow in. These are your *reactive strategies* – things we do once we feel our stress levels are rising. This is a bit like poking some holes in the bottom of your cup to help the water flow out in a safe and sustainable way. We'll revisit these in more detail in Chapter 6 when we look at rest, but, for now, we can separate these into two camps: regulators (short term) and routines (long term).

REGULATORS (SHORT TERM)

- Body scan
- Box breathing
- Guided meditation
- Playing 'categories'
- 5–4–3–2–1 technique
- Changing your environment
- Progressive muscle relaxation

ROUTINES (LONG TERM)

- Gratitude
- Journalling
- Mind-dumping
- Positive reframing

- Taking a short walk

- Verbalising your thoughts

- Using the thought court

> *Many of us have been running all our lives. Practise*
> *stopping.*
> *Thich Nhat Hanh, 1991*

BOOMERANGS AND SLINGSHOTS

It is important to say that some of the things you're currently doing for your stress or mental health might actually be doing more harm than good; we need to address the elephants in the room.

 HINTS AND TIPS 3.1

When overused, some of our stress management strategies might become more like crutches than foundations.

It's fine to have coping strategies that serve the purpose of self-soothing: the soak in the bath, the glass of wine, the takeaway. These things can increase the levels of dopamine, our reward and motivation chemical (more on this shortly), and can bring us a sense of control and pleasure. But these can quickly become boomerangs: they're easy to do, you feel like the stress has gone, but quite quickly they come whipping back round to knock you on the back of the head. As always though, the danger is in the dose.

Examples of slingshots:

- prepping lunch

- paying a bill

- exercising.

Examples of boomerangs:

- having a drink

- getting a takeaway

- binging TV.

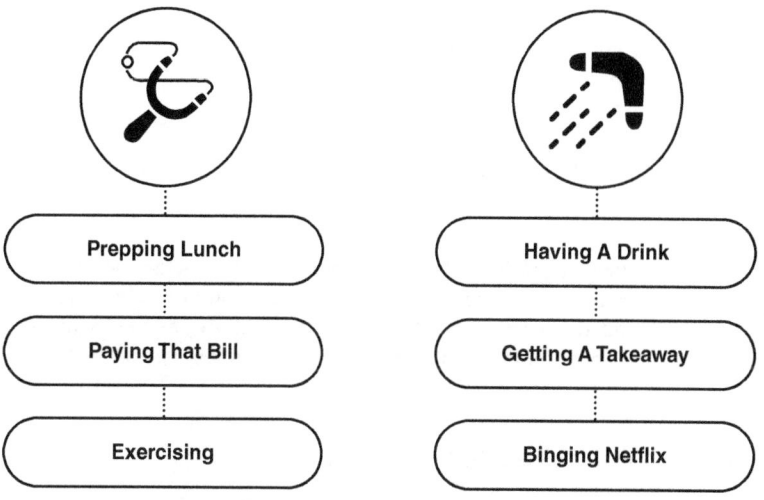

Prepping Lunch	Having A Drink
Paying That Bill	Getting A Takeaway
Exercising	Binging Netflix

Figure 3.1

With slingshots, although they take more effort in the short term, once you let them go the stress is actually managed. It might be preparing your breakfast, paying that bill that's been hanging over your head or going for that walk or workout. You exchange short-term discomfort for long-term benefit.

To summarise, when you're tired, stressed or overwhelmed, it's easy to seek out comfort, pleasure and instant gratification to feel better. However, when it comes to stress, the phrase 'easy choices, hard life; hard choices, easy life' rings particularly true.

 # REFLECTION 3.2

Think about your self-care behaviours for a moment. Do they tend to fall into true self-care (slingshots) or are you leaning more towards self-soothing (boomerangs)?

 # HINTS AND TIPS 3.2

Remember that self-soothing behaviours absolutely have their place; I'm a big fan of a bubble bath. But, ultimately, if we're really wanting to build healthier coping strategies, we might need to place more of our attention on the slingshot behaviours.

YOUR MENTAL HEALTH MENU

By far the most popular framework I share with clients and schools is my *mental health menu*. This structure builds on what we've spoken about and can serve as a great second level, or alternative lens through which to view your mentally healthy habits.

The mental health menu doesn't just focus on managing the stressors of day-to-day life; it dives deeper into understanding the four chemicals most influential on our mood and mental health, and how we can increase them in realistic, manageable ways. Those four chemicals are dopamine, oxytocin, serotonin and endorphins.

- *Dopamine*: often slightly misunderstood as just our reward chemical, dopamine also helps us feel focused, motivated and optimistic.

- *Oxytocin*: our love and connection chemical that's responsible for bonding, trust and a sense of belonging. Key for our mental health and something many struggle with.

- *Serotonin*: dubbed the 'happiness hormone', serotonin is responsible for our mood and a sense of calmness.

- *Endorphins*: the brain's natural pain and stress reliever. Built to not only help us through the tough times, be that mentally or physically, but also to feel great because of them.

I know what you might be thinking: *'That's great, Charlie! But I'm already stressed, I have no time and I have even less headspace to think about four more things I've got to do every day. How does this help me?'* Well, this is where the menu concept comes in …

When you eat out at a restaurant or order a takeaway, do you feel you need to order the whole menu (and finish it) to feel like you've satisfied your hunger and had an enjoyable experience? Of course you don't! You browse the menu, think about how hungry you are, what you fancy and maybe even how much time you've got to eat it. We can apply that 'menu mentality' to our mental health too. We can break things down into bitesize chunks so that they feel manageable and realistic – even if you've got just a few minutes to support yourself.

Notice how it's broken down into time periods? This is going to be key when thinking about how we can increase these four chemicals. As teachers, we don't often have half an hour to exercise – or even half an hour to take a lunch break, come to think of it. We need to be realistic and practical, otherwise we'll set our expectations too high and set ourselves up for failure, further reinforcing those internal self stories of *'I can't do it'* and *'It's not possible as a teacher.'*

Table 3.1 offers an example of a mental health menu.

Table 3.1   Mental health menu

	<5 minutes	5–15 minutes	15+ minutes
Dopamine *Motivation*	Splash cold water on your face	Give the house a quick hoover	Go phone free for 30 minutes
	Clean/tidy a room quickly	Go for a 10-minute walk	Set a timer and focus on a task
	Make your bed	Sit and read for 15 minutes	Cook a quick meal
Oxytocin *Bonding*	Smile at a stranger	Organise a fun activity with friends	Have a cuddle in front of the TV
	Give a loved one a hug	Listen attentively when in conversation	Spend time with friends phone free
	Write what went well		
	Practise gratitude		
Serotonin *Mood*	Listen to a meditation	Go for a 10-minute walk in daylight	Cook and eat a nutritious meal
	Practise box breathing (4,4,4,4x10)	Complete a 10-minute meditation	Practise a wind-down routine
	Have a glass of water	Listen to a nature soundscape	Get a good night's sleep
	Mind-dump onto paper		
Endorphins *Pain relief*	Dance around to your favourite songs	Complete a short workout	Watch an episode of something funny
	Sing loudly to your favourite songs	Try a contrast shower (hot to cold)	Have a laugh with some friends
	Try a 5-minute stretching routine	10 squats, 10 lunges, 10 burpees x 3	Complete an intense workout

 # REFLECTION 3.3

Create your own mental health menu. You can use the example in Table 3.1 to get you started or refer to the resources at the back of the book to give you some more ideas.

Try to think about what you really enjoy doing and, as always, keep it super simple.

NOTE IT DOWN

Have a look at the capacity cup model above. First, in one colour, write what you're currently doing to build boundaries and to be proactive and reactive with your stress. Then, in a second colour, add the strategies you'd like to build in from what we've covered so far, and the rest of this chapter.

Boundaries:

Preventative strategies:

Reactive strategies:

CHAPTER 4
HOW CAN I EAT WELL – EASILY?

This chapter explores the ideas that:

- our relationship with food and the way we think about it are as important as what we put on our plates for our mental and physical health
- keeping our nutrition super simple is a lost art and something we'd all benefit from doing more of
- eating well doesn't need to be expensive or time-consuming; there are easy ways to make managing our food more efficient as teachers.

NUTRITION AND WELLBEING

When it comes to wellbeing, nutrition holds a special place in my heart. It was the first area I really grew passionate about and was subsequently the first area I decided to study, qualifying as a nutrition coach back in 2019. At the time of writing this chapter, in mid-2024, the world of nutrition has become even more complicated, with an influx of extremist social media accounts sharing what can only be described as damaging diet dogma.

As I write this, I've just paused to search the word 'diet' on a few different social media platforms; here are just a few of the headlines that have come up.

- *Bread is bad!*

- *Is your cereal killing you?*

- *Only eat like your ancestors*

- *Big-Food has you addicted …*

- *Forget the fruit, only eat meat*

- And even, *Why water is ruining your health …*

Now, I don't know about you, but after reading that I feel confused and overwhelmed.

MANAGING OUR MENTAL HEALTH AROUND EATING WELL

As a former teacher and now a nutritionist, I'm in a unique position. I understand the challenges we can have around food as educators and also the *(actual)* science behind what helps us feel great, mentally and physically. Whenever I talk, write or support my clients with their nutrition, I keep one framework in mind: KIPPERS. Ironically, I'm not much of a fan of fish.

Keep

It

Practical

Personal

Enjoyable

Realistic

Simple

It's so important that we don't get bogged down in 'perfection' when it comes to our food, especially in a profession that can sometimes subconsciously promote perfectionism. Everything falls on a spectrum from less optimal to more optimal – we can always be 'better' with our habits, but if this is at the detriment of our mental health, then is it really healthy?

It's got to work for us, our nutritional needs, our brain and body. Some people feel amazing on a high carbohydrate lunch, but most of us will feel a bit sluggish afterwards. Some feel fine without breakfast whereas a lot of us find ourselves flagging come 10am. Nutrition is incredibly nuanced and personal; there's no 'right' or 'wrong'. The big one that doesn't often get a look-in is our own enjoyment. Contrary to popular belief, we don't just eat for fuel, we eat for fun too, so being aware of this and using food to nourish ourselves emotionally and socially is also important.

Finally, it's got to be realistic, which often means simple – especially for us as those working in schools. We quite often eat on the go and don't have a lot of time to spend planning, shopping and preparing overly complicated, Michelin star-style meals.

So, *KIPPERS* is basically all the things diet culture, quick-fix fads and slimming clubs get us to avoid. Can you tell I've got a bit of a bee in my bonnet about diet dogma in general? So, with that in mind, let's look at a few practical frameworks that can *actually* help you regain control and finally feel confident again around food, without damaging your relationship with it or your mental health.

Let's start with the most simple, and work our way up in complexity …

FRAMEWORK #1: THE 5−3−1 APPROACH

As I strive to simplify nutrition and make it as manageable for teachers as possible, I keep coming up against one inevitable truth: as teachers we typically don't have much time to give to what we eat. So, in the beginning, the simpler the approach, the better. The 5−3−1 is as easy to implement as it is to remember. Each day, aim to eat:

5 fruits and veggies – think plants; to build on this, aim to eat a rainbow

3 portions of protein – think meat, fish, dairy, eggs, legumes (beans, peas, pulses)

1 food that you *really* enjoy – this is to promote moderation and a positive relationship with all food.

 REFLECTION 4.1

What could the 5−3−1 approach look like in a day in your life?

 HINTS AND TIPS 4.1

There are two techniques I find work really well with increasing the amount of fruits and vegetables in our diets:

1. **split them across your meals and snacks, so it could be berries with breakfast, a banana at breaktime, some salad with lunch and some onions and peppers with dinner**

2. **hide them in saucy dishes, like chilli con carne, spaghetti bolognese, soups, stews and curries; finely chop, grate, blend or mash them in and you'll barely notice.**

FRAMEWORK #2: THE FOOD FLOW

Building on the 5–3–1 approach, the *food flow* is a really practical way for us to simplify how we think about our food; it works great when meal planning or serving your own food at a buffet. It goes like this:

Protein → Fruits and veggies → Carbohydrates → Healthy Fats

The flow is in this order to help prioritise the things we're often lacking in our diet (protein and plants), especially in our modern food environment which has an over-availability of affordable, highly processed and easy-to-overeat foods.

When planning meals, start with protein. You've probably heard a lot about protein and for good reason. It's one of the three primary macronutrients (nutrients we need in larger amounts) alongside carbohydrates and fats. Protein supports muscle repair and growth, immune function and even weight management by helping us feel fuller for longer and less likely to overeat. Protein helps us with: hormone production, bone health, metabolism, blood sugar stabilisation, energy and even improving the quality of our hair, skin and nails. To get more protein, you can eat foods such as meat, fish, eggs, dairy or plant-based sources like beans, chickpeas, or soy products like tofu.

 REFLECTION 4.2

What are your favourite protein sources? List three to five and use them as your foundation for most of your meals. It might help to split them into breakfast, lunch and dinner sources.

Moving onto our fruits and vegetables. Now, I'm not going to tell you that you need to eat your veggies (you know that already), but I do want to highlight just how far-reaching the impact of eating some more plants can be. Fruits and veggies are often high in fibre, helping us with things like weight management by increasing satiety, stabilising blood sugar and reducing calorie intake. They're packed full of what we call *micronutrients* (vitamins and minerals). These are the nutrients our bodies need in smaller amounts. Fruit and veg supports us with immune function, digestion, hydration, skin health, heart health, brain health – all the *healths* really! The list of benefits is too long to list here. In short, if you're wanting to feel your best, increase your energy and maintain a healthy mind and body, you need to make sure you're eating your five-a-day.

 ## REFLECTION 4.3

What are your favourite fruits and vegetables? List five to eight and add them into most of your meals, or have them as snacks. Again, split them into breakfast, lunch and dinner sources.

Next up are our carbohydrates (I call these the vehicle of your meal; they drive your energy and often provide a frame for the rest of the meal – for example, a pasta dish, a wrap or a pizza). Many of us have been told that carbohydrates can lead to weight gain; this is simply not true. Weight gain is a product of consuming more energy (calories) than our body is using, on average, over an extended period of time. Carbohydrates can be simple or complex. Both are useful and both, in moderation, can be part of a broad and balanced diet. Simple carbs come from sources like some fruits (e.g. grapes, apples or oranges), dairy products like milk or foods with added sugars like sweets, ice-cream or chocolate. Complex carbohydrates can be found in foods such as grains, starchy vegetables (like potatoes) and beans.

REFLECTION 4.4

What are your carbohydrates? Pasta? Rice? Wraps? Oats? Bananas? List three to five and use them as the frame of your main meals, especially lunches and dinners.

Finally, the flow finishes with healthy fats. Fat is another nutrient that has got a bad rap over the years, but is linked to many health benefits, when you consume the right types: heart health, brain health and even absorption of certain vitamins and minerals. Bottom line: we need fats to feel our best. You can add healthy fats into your diet with foods such as olive oil, coconut oil, avocado, nuts, seeds and fatty fish. The majority of us would also benefit from moderating certain fat sources, like full-fat dairy, butter and fatty cuts of meat.

REFLECTION 4.5

What healthy fats can you factor in? List two to three and add them into at least one meal a day. Again, split them into breakfast, lunch and dinner sources if you can.

FRAMEWORKS #3 AND #4: THE PORTION PLATE AND HAND MODEL OF PORTION CONTROL

Using the food flow is great for simplifying what we put on our plates, but how much of each group do we need? While nutrition is a very personal science – and, of course, when using the following models, it will come down to things like the size of your plates, how accurately you eyeball your portions, etcetera – there are some frameworks we can use to guide us in the right direction.

With clients, I like to begin with two visuals. The first is the *portion plate*. Really simply, when serving your food, aim to have around ¼ of your plate as protein, ¼ as carbohydrates, about ⅓–½ as fruits and vegetables and then a small amount of healthy fats.

The second framework is the *hand model of portion control*. At your main meals, aim to have a palm-size portion of protein, two cupped handfuls of vegetables, one cupped handful of carbohydrates (like dry pasta or dry rice – before cooking) and then a thumb's worth of healthy fats. This will work out roughly the same as the portion plate. Again, nutrition is incredibly individual and no one-size-fits-all approach will ever tick all the boxes, but these frameworks aim to get you a simple starting point to managing your diet.

THE 3FS: UNDERSTANDING WHY WE EAT

Remember, we don't just eat for fuel. As humans, we have a strong social connection with food. It often features as the focal point of our events, meetings and celebrations – and it has done so for thousands of years. We also have emotional connections with our food: we go out to eat to celebrate a promotion, we enjoy cake at birthday parties and we often offer sustenance in the form of a cup of tea and a biscuit when someone has been given difficult news.

 HINTS AND TIPS 4.2

There are actually three primary reasons we eat: for fuel, for fun or eating that is flagging something (usually via an emotion that's risen from an unmet need).

But sometimes, especially as teachers, we can lean on food as a coping strategy. It can provide us with a sense of certainty, control or some much-needed comfort after an emotionally challenging day. This is okay as long as it's in moderation and we have a wider range of stress management strategies to rely on. Now we're not going to go into emotion-led eating or relationships with food too much in this book, we're focusing on habits after all. But if you feel like maybe your eating is led by emotion a little too often and it's impacting your health, or your relationship with food, I've got a really simple strategy for you.

THE PAUSE PRINCIPLE

One of the core reasons we find it difficult to eat well, whatever that means for us personally, is that most of us live in overabundant food environments. I don't know about you but if I open my kitchen cupboards, food literally falls out. Alongside adapting our environments to support us in making the choices around our food that we'd like to, we can also look at ways of interrupting the habit loops (remember these from Chapter 1?) we've built around certain foods.

The best way to do this is to use the *pause principle*. To give some context, let me quickly explain where the principle fits into my *respond vs react* model, built on the habit work of B.J. Fogg, Charles Duhigg and James Clear. Simply put, before we decide to reach and grab that food, there is a cue. It might be a time of day, an emotion, a location, our energy levels, an event from the day – or maybe a combination of all of these. Following that cue, a strong craving rises and, usually, we react almost instantly. Although our brain then perceives a reward, we also experience the heavy, dull ache of regret and a negative relationship with that food, the emotion and ourselves.

Cue → Craving → Reaction → Reward and regret

But, with the pause principle, we can pattern interrupt this cycle. We can create space (or pause) between the cue and our reaction; we can turn reaction into response by simply taking a few seconds. So, next time that craving arises and you grab that food from the cupboard, try placing it on the side and stepping back for just 60 seconds. Some people like to stand

and wait, some like to change rooms, some even go for a walk – simply create space. Once the time has passed and you've re-engaged the logical, consequence-conscious part of your brain, you can then make a more rational choice around that food.

By doing this we strengthen connections and responses between certain parts of our brains that are responsible for emotional regulation, decision-making, planning and habit formation. It also floods our brains with feel-good chemicals, like dopamine. This means that the more we practise pausing, and responding rather than reacting, the better at it we get.

Cue → Craving → Pause → Response → Real reward

THE TEN QUICK COOK COMMANDMENTS

As we begin to wrap up this chapter, I want to share with you my *ten quick cook commandments*, my guidelines for eating well with ease. These ideas are here to help make planning, preparing and polishing off your meals (and snacks) as simple and straightforward as possible.

1. *Five-minute meal planner*

    One of the keys to eating well is planning ahead – boring but true. Consider using a five-minute meal plan template to map out your meals for the week. Having a plan in place can help you make more optimal food choices *and* enjoy the foods you love.

2. Batch cooking

    Time is tight for us as teachers and batch cooking can be a lifesaver. You could spend 30 minutes prepping meals that can last for three days. This not only saves time but also ensures you have nutritious options readily available when you need them.

3. Prep breakfast as dinner cooks

   So simple it's barely a tip. While in the kitchen sorting dinner, make breakfast for the next day. Overnight oats or a layered yoghurt pot with fresh fruit can be quick and filling options.

4. Go frozen

   Frozen food often gets a bad rap, but it can be a convenient and nutritious option. Frozen fruits and vegetables are often more nutritious than fresh ones and can be used in a pinch. Plus, they're cheaper and have a longer shelf life, reducing food waste.

5. Apply your appliances

   Make the most of your kitchen appliances to save time and effort. Multitask by using the oven, hob, air fryer, or slow cooker to prepare multiple meals at the same time. My go to is sticking a traybake in the oven, something in the slow cooker and using the wok on the hob. More meals, same time.

6. Cooking double

   Sometimes, the simplest solutions are the best. Cook larger portions and enjoy leftovers for another meal. For example, a pot of chilli can be eaten for lunch the next day or frozen to eat later.

7. Use a base

   Simplify your meals by using a single ingredient base – for example, mince-meat and a tin of chopped tomatoes. With a few added ingredients and seasonings, you can turn it into a chilli, bolognese, curry, or even tacos.

8. Pick pre-prepped

   In a pinch, pre-prepped ingredients like microwaveable rice, sauces, sandwiches and even fresh ready meals can be a lifesaver. Are they ideal to have every day? Probably not. But when you're tight for time they can help you make more optimal choices with your food compared to the alternative.

9. Batch prepare and portion

   I've borrowed this from one of my amazing clients. Save time during the week by pre-cutting ingredients like veggies and meats. Portion them out in advance to make cooking quicker and more convenient Monday to Friday.

10.   One-pot wonders

Simplify your cooking routine with one-pot meals like traybakes, curries, soups and stews. These dishes are not only easy to prepare, but also minimise cleanup, saving you even more time.

NOTE IT DOWN

Choose one to three of the ten commandment strategies listed above to trial next week. Jot down here which ones you will try and for which meals. Come back to this as you plan and prepare your meals for the week. They really will save you hours.

CHAPTER 5

HOW CAN I MAKE MOVEMENT WORK FOR ME?

This chapter explores the following ideas:

- simply focusing on small ways we can move our body more can bring us many of the physical and mental benefits of exercise
- the term 'exercise' can come with tricky connotations for many of us and can damage the way we think about our movement, our health and our bodies
- movement plays a powerful part in managing mental health.

THINKING ABOUT EXERCISE

 REFLECTION 5.1

How do you feel about exercise at the moment? Do you enjoy it? Do you do it consistently? Take a few moments to jot down some thoughts around your relationship with movement; this'll be important to come back to later.

One area a lot of teachers tell me they struggle with once term time kicks in is exercise. For some, the holidays are a respite from the busyness of work and allow them to kickstart their routines, but when school life takes over, it's the first thing to go. For others it's the opposite: the routine of the week actually makes exercise easier but, again, once they reach a pinch point in the academic year or their energy falls off a cliff, so does their movement. It's safe to say, I've been there.

THE MOVEMENT MINDSET

Before we go any further, I want to offer you one simple mindset shift that genuinely changed the way I think about exercise: *I stopped exercising.*

Okay, that's not strictly true, but I changed my language around it. I ditched the term 'exercise' and all the negative connotations and pressure it put on me and I swapped it for two others: 'movement' and 'training'. For so many of us, exercise comes with baggage. Memories of smelly school changing rooms, running laps in the freezing cold or running on a treadmill for an hour for the sole purpose of burning calories. It's no wonder we struggle to keep consistent with it. Movement and training, however, are *different*.

Let's start with training. For me, and the teachers I coach, training is purposeful. It's productive. It promotes positive thoughts and emotions, rather than the dread of, 'Ergh, back to the treadmill,' that so many of us have experienced. What makes training is the fact that it has a direction or goal and you're taking progressive steps toward it – and seeing the change: feeling less tired after a workout, lifting heavier weights or running that 2km loop a little bit quicker. It doesn't have to be training alone though. Maybe you enjoy going with a close friend to a *clubbercise* class for fun or challenging yourself by joining an advanced yoga class (anyone who thinks yoga is just stretching and humming has another thing coming – it's hard work). It fulfils one gap that exercise quite often doesn't: it has purpose ... and that extends far beyond the physical as we'll discuss shortly.

Movement is a little more gentle; it's relaxed – and you probably already do more of it than you think. It might be parking your car further away and walking. It could be walking the long way round to the photocopier or leaving some printing there so you have to do a couple of trips. Or maybe it's even touching your toes and reaching to the ceiling while the kettle is boiling! Some people like to track their steps, others just go by feel. Now, as a teacher, there will absolutely be days that don't go to plan. We need to accept this to some degree and know that sometimes our exercise will be affected. On these days, just focusing on moving more in the time that you have can really help – plus it can give you so many of the brain and body benefits we associate with training. Let's talk about that ...

WHY MOVE MORE?

I could spend the rest of this book talking about the benefits of movement alone. As someone who aims to walk most mornings and trains maybe three to five times a week (mostly a mixture of running and weight training at the moment), if I don't move or train for a few days I feel a marked difference in myself. It's amazing how much better I feel just moving more. But for years I had no idea of these benefits. For years I sat on a goldmine of ways to help my mental health and didn't even realise. Most of these benefits can be linked back to a few key brain chemicals which featured as our all-star cast in Chapter 3. But let's give them a quick recap, and introduce a couple of newbies, in case you've skipped ahead to this chapter.

- *Dopamine*: a neurotransmitter that helps us to feel rewarded, motivated and focused. Dopamine is part of the *runner's high* that the runner in your life is always going on about.

- *BDNF*: a protein that helps us with learning, brain health and offsetting neurodegenerative diseases like Alzheimer's.

- *Serotonin*: another neurotransmitter that supports our sleep, improves our mood and can even reduce symptoms of depression and anxiety.

- *Endorphins*: these chemicals are your brain's natural painkillers helping manage stress and later reducing feelings of tension and anxiety. They play a key part in that runner's high.

- *Anandamide*: this one's a bit fancy and a little less known. As endocannabinoids, these molecules help us feel in a state of 'bliss', helping in regulating mood, pain, hunger and memory.

The best part? Most of these benefits can be felt from something as simple as walking outside, at a slightly increased pace, for as little as 15 minutes.

THE MICROMOVEMENT METHOD

During times like planning, preparation and assessment (PPA), meetings and sometimes even in lessons, it's easy for us to go hours without moving much – and thus feeling the opposite of many of the benefits we just discussed. This is especially true for colleagues who might office-based, or have long commutes as part of their working day. It's also true that, for a lot of us teachers, time genuinely is short. The myth of 'we all have the same 24 hours in the day' that's spouted around the fitness industry doesn't really ring true when you're responsible for 20–30 young people for six hours a day – and the rest.

To help with this, I've designed the concept of *movement multipliers*. These are realistic, manageable ways to increase your movement, your energy and lift your mood. Think of them as short, sharp breaks you can use to move your body and begin to feel those benefits. The idea here is, as always, to keep it simple. Don't overthink these. Here's an example of how you could use movement multipliers throughout your day:

- *upon waking*: stretch your body while waiting for the kettle to boil or for the shower to warm up

- *while teaching*: tango-teach! Make sure to move: walk if you can or move your arms and gesticulate

- *breaktime*: take the long way round to the staffroom or take a two-minute lap of the playground

- *movement break*: for the children, and for you. Just two to three movements to shake out the body will help

- *lunchtime*: go for a ten-minute walk with a colleague, or on your own

- *before dinner*: try a ten-minute training session – a brief bodyweight workout that requires no equipment (see Chapter 6).

Already this individual would have moved their body for 30+ minutes – and a lot more in-between those more formal movement breaks. Imagine how this stacks up over a week, a month or a term. The compound interest of this movement will be huge.

NOTE IT DOWN

LET'S DESIGN YOUR OWN MICROMOVEMENT PLANNER.
MENTALLY REPLAY A TYPICAL DAY IN YOUR LIFE AND LOOK
FOR OPPORTUNITIES FOR MOVEMENT.

IS THERE A PHONE CALL YOU COULD TAKE WHILE
WALKING? A CHANCE TO STRETCH WHILE WATCHING TV?
A POINT IN THE TEACHING DAY YOU COULD JOIN IN WITH
THE CHILDREN'S MOVEMENT OR A CHANCE TO BRING MORE
MOVEMENT INTO A LESSON?

USE THIS SPACE TO JOT DOWN SOME OPPORTUNITIES FOR
MOVEMENT YOU HAVE FOUND IN YOUR DAY/WEEK.

CHAPTER 6
HOW CAN I REST AND RECOVER MORE EFFECTIVELY?

This chapter explores the ideas that:

- no matter how passionate you are, you are still human. You are not a superhero or an infinite resource that'll never run out; rest is productive
- there are seven types of rest; we can break these down into small behaviours and habits that fit into our everyday lives
- sleep is one of the most powerful things we can do for our overall health and longevity; it's truly the first foundation.

YOU'RE NOT A SUPERHERO

Rest is not idle, not wasteful.
Sometimes rest is the most productive thing you can do.
Erica Layne, 2019

As teachers we want to help. It's why we chose this career. Fundamentally, we want to leave people better off than when we found them. But one trap I see teachers fall into, and it's a trap I fell into myself for many years, is expecting their brains and bodies to simply keep going no matter how much stress and strain they put them under. I think this is, at least in part, due to the fact that life in school is simply just so busy; we often don't take a second to take stock of just how much we're putting ourselves through and how far removed that is from what we're actually built to do. It's no wonder burnout, chronic fatigue and illness can catch us unawares.

And I'm sorry to say, you're *not* a superhero.

This narrative that teachers are superheroes, not limited by human needs, reinforces the belief that we can simply keep going, no matter the cost; that we can't take a break because the fate of our world depends on us – like a superhero. But the truth is, you are human. You have a finite mental and physical capacity. Without respecting that it's going to be a one-way ticket to burnout.

UNDERSTANDING REST

It's important to define our terms when we're talking about rest. This is the best definition I've come across; it encompasses so much.

*Rest is, quite simply, when you stop using a part
of you that's used up, worn out, damaged, or inflamed,
so that it has a chance to renew itself.*
Emily Nagoski, 2019

There are many models for rest, but my favourite is Dr Saundra Dalton-Smith's *7 Types of Rest* (n.d.). Dr Dalton-Smith proposes that there are seven different areas of rest we'd benefit from being mindful of (if you feel like that's already a lot to be thinking about, don't worry – I'm going to simplify them). They are:

- *physical rest*:

    ○ active physical: stretching, massage, yoga, gentle walking

    ○ passive physical: sleeping, napping, lying down

- *mental rest*: brain breaks, mindfulness, brain boundaries

- *emotional rest*: sharing emotions, journalling, processing

- *sensory rest*: screen breaks, calming music, quiet spaces, low lighting

- *creative rest*: walking in nature, appreciating art, creative activities

- *spiritual rest*: connecting with a larger purpose, e.g. church or a cause

- *social rest*: being with loved ones, energising interactions, clubs and groups.

As you look through that list, there might be some you can spot that you already do regularly, there might also be some you save for half-terms or holidays – I know that was what I found.

REFLECTION 6.1

Let's audit those areas on a *weekly* basis. How regularly, and for how long, do you get rest in each of these areas? Which would you like to give more attention in your life?

YOUR REST MINDSET

I want to take a moment to quickly reframe rest with you. Most of us have been taught to view rest as something that happens at the end of the day, week or maybe even half-term. It's the thing we do *if* we get enough time, and if we think we deserve it. I want to challenge that with a different model.

HINTS AND TIPS 6.1

Rest isn't the opposite of being productive, it's *part* of being productive; just as recharging your phone at night is part of using it the next day.

Rest comes first in the productivity cycle – begin with rest. And, just to quickly touch on productivity, that marking, planning or application that takes you three hours at 11pm at night when you're absolutely exhausted would likely take you a third of that time, and be much better quality, if you simply let yourself rest.

I fully understand how difficult it can be to even take a lunch break some days, let alone take time to rest during the school day. But it really doesn't need to take hours and it definitely doesn't need to wait till the end of the day, week or half-term.

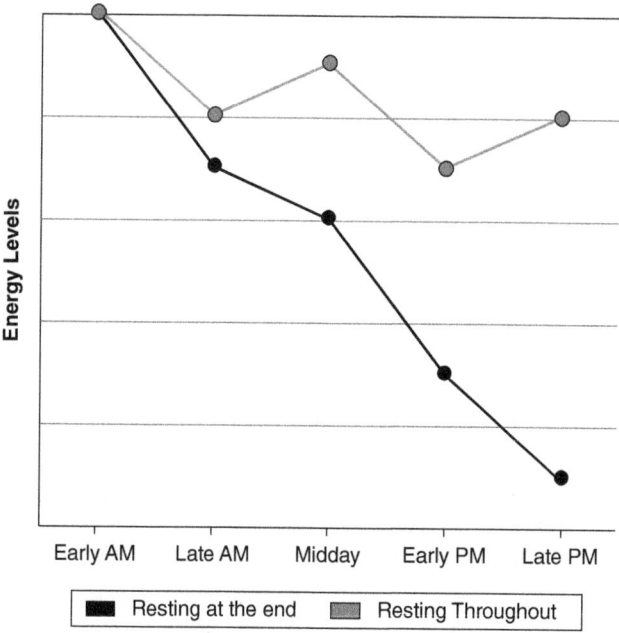

Figure 6.1

DAILY DECOMPRESSIONS

Another concept that I've developed is the idea of *daily decompressions*. What's great about these is that they take just a few moments, don't require any equipment and can be done anywhere. They work best when you tag them onto an existing part of your day – for example, as you pull up at work or after the children go out to breaktime. The one thing that they all have in common is that they aim to help you regulate your central nervous system and calm your brain and body. Below are a few examples.

- *Body scan*: starting at the top of your head, scan your way down your body checking in for any tension and release the muscle as you breathe.

- *Box breathing*: you can start with a 3:3:3:3 pace, breathe in through your nose for three seconds, hold your breath for three seconds, exhale through pursed lips for three seconds and hold again for three seconds. Repeat as necessary.

- *Guided meditation*: there are plenty available for free on YouTube™, but Headspace™ offers free membership for educators; you'll just need proof of employment.

- *Listing loves*: this is a great technique. Simply spend a few minutes listing things you love and/or are grateful for. With clients I recommend the 5Ps: people, places, passions, positive experiences and times you've persevered.

- *5–4–3–2–1 technique*: a popular grounding technique credited to psychotherapist Betty Alice Erickon. Simply focus on five things you can see, four things you can touch, three things you can hear, two things you can smell and one thing you can taste (or an extra thing you can touch).

- *Changing your environment*: the role of getting a change of scene can't be overstated in shifting your state. The movement, exposure to daylight, increased breathing and even the widening of your field of vision are unbelievably powerful in helping the brain and body regulate and rest.

HINTS AND TIPS 6.2

Known as *horizon gazing,* going outside to view an open area allows your field of vision to widen, sparking a cascade of physiological effects in the body: it relaxes the eyes, encourages perspective, increases dopamine and serotonin. It even reduces our brain's *fight or flight* response, helping our brains and bodies to move towards the *rest and digest* state.

SELF-FIRST NOT SELFISH

Another struggle we can have in the way we think about rest is feeling that anything that gives to us is taking away from others; but this is a flawed thought process. We want to help. We want to leave people better than when we found them, so giving ourselves time and space can feel contradictory to that; it can feel selfish. But this is where reality defies logic and a short-term mindset can be our undoing.

Yes, in the explicit moment where you set a boundary or delay giving to others in order to protect your own wellbeing, your needs are coming ahead of theirs; that's true. But this isn't selfish, it's self-first. And by resting and recovering now, you're able to give others the best possible version of yourself later. Don't forget you deserve to feel your best too, just by virtue of being here. To make this really clear, let's imagine the alternative; this might ring all too true for you: you give and you give until you've got nothing left. You suffer and you actually end up giving much less to others in the long term. Constantly giving has diminishing returns.

To add to this, I know a lot of teachers struggle with feeling 'enough': good enough, like they've done enough, like they are enough. In many countries, the systems we work in are built on continuous accountability, assessment and improvement, which can contribute to that feeling of never quite being good enough. For me, it was also something I brought into teaching from my younger years and I tried to use teaching as a tool to fill that gap. It didn't work. Teaching, by nature, is a bottomless pit. You can keep going and going and you'll never 'complete' teaching. If we can reframe what we first think about rest, we can approach it with an entirely new outlook.

 REFLECTION 6.2

What does the phrase 'good enough' mean to you in terms of teaching? Write a description of what a week would look like for someone who is doing 'enough'.

SUPPORTING YOUR SLEEP

> *Rest is the golden chain that binds health and our bodies.*
> *Thomas Dekker (Deckar, n.d.)*

I know earlier I said that rest isn't all about getting your eight hours (that model is a bit of a myth anyway), but when talking about recovery, we can't ignore sleep. Like it or not, the late night TV binges and doom scrolling when you can't drift off are having a much more detrimental impact on your sleep, and therefore your mental and physical health, than you might like to think.

Poor sleep has been linked to reduced focus and memory retention, increased stress, anxiety and depression, a weakened immune system, increased risk of heart disease, diabetes and obesity, hormonal imbalances, reduced emotional regulation and fluctuations in appetite and metabolism. These are just some direct impacts; imagine the hundreds of indirect impacts these symptoms of poor sleep could cause across your mental and physical health. In fact, if you were to stay awake for as little as 19 hours (that's you waking up at 6am and still being awake at 1am), your attention and ability to think is the same as if you were legally drunk! It's safe to say, if there's anywhere to focus on your health first and foremost, it's worth starting with sleep.

 REFLECTION 6.3

Before we begin, take a moment to just reflect on your sleep routines and habits. Consider the key areas below. What would you score yourself for each? (1–10, with 10 being the best approach you can take.)

- **Your sleep and wake times**

- **Your sunlight exposure**

- **Your caffeine intake**

- **Your work curfew**

- **Your sleep environment**

- **Your wind-down routine**

- **Your screen time.**

THE REST SLEEP SYSTEM

As with anything, we could get incredibly granular with sleep, but I want to give you a simple, straightforward system that will help you take small steps in improving this all-important area of rest. Introducing the *REST sleep system* ...

REGULAR ROUTINES

Our sleep is largely governed by our circadian rhythms, often referred to as our *body clock*. These rhythms impact everything from when we concentrate best, our body temperature, hormonal changes, hunger to when we feel sleepy, even our physical strength and endurance. The best way to regulate our circadian rhythm is to keep to consistent routines. Consider:

- going to bed and waking up at a similar time – *parents, I know this can be tough!*

- keeping meal times and breaks as consistent as you can

- getting some sunlight as early in the day as possible, even for just a few minutes

- cutting caffeine after lunchtime, it has a three- to five-hour half-life meaning drinking a strong coffee with 100mg of caffeine before that 4pm meeting would leave you with around 25mg in your system at 2am!

EVOLVING EVENINGS

One area we often struggle with as teachers is winding down adequately before bed. We might work late or delay sleep so we can feel like we've had a moment for ourselves. Despite the most recent research showing that bluelight from our screens isn't quite as detrimental to our sleep as once thought, it still isn't ideal. Think about:

- adjusting your evening meal so you're not going to be too full or too hungry

- taking space from screens for 60 minutes before bed where possible

- setting yourself a strict work curfew or laptop limit; protect your peace

- remove or limit notifications, apps and chats on your devices

- have a designated wind-down activity – breathing, journalling and soundscapes are great.

SLEEP SPACES

The environment in which we sleep massively impacts not just the quality, but also the quantity of our sleep. There are some simple guidelines you can tick off to make sure you've created a supportive sleep space:

- keep your room as quiet and dark as possible

- make sure your bedding is clean and comfortable

- crack a window to try and keep your bedroom cool

- charge your phone away from your bed

- avoid TVs and screens in the bedroom.

TROUBLESHOOTING TIPS

If you've gradually built these into your day, and you've kept consistent for a while, but you're struggling to sleep, there are a few areas we can troubleshoot before you might want to speak to your GP or a sleep professional:

- if your brain is busy, try writing your thoughts out about an hour or so before bed; it can help you feel like the issue has been 'parked' for the night

- if you can't sleep, don't stay in bed tossing and turning; we want to maintain a positive sleep association with your bed. Keep your environment sleepy, but take yourself to another room, for example

- you can try supplements; most of these include a combination of ingredients like zinc, magnesium, tryptophan, chamomile, tart cherry extract and ashwagandha. You can also speak to your GP or pharmacist about supplementing melatonin, the sleep hormone.

NOTE IT DOWN

Build your own REST sleep system using some of the ideas shared above. For now, concentrate on just one tweak in each area and focus on embedding these for at least a month before looking to make any further changes. Small steps compound over time.

Regular routines:

Evolving evenings:

Sleep space:

Troubleshooting:

SUMMARY

*Every action you take is a vote for the type of
person you wish to become.*
James Clear, 2018

As we come to the end of this *Little Guide*, I want to take a moment to thank you for putting the time aside to be here, for reading through these pages and prioritising yourself and your health. Putting you first isn't selfish, it's self-first. I understand that it's not easy to do as a teacher, and it might not come naturally; I know it didn't for me. However, there's arguably nothing more impactful when you're trying to make a difference to others.

Know that these changes we've outlined will take time and it won't always be an easy road (the mantra of *'Forward, not straight'* comes to mind). In those times where school takes over, life kicks you when you're down or the fog of term-time starts to set in, I'd like you to do just one thing: pause. Just take a moment, step back, close your eyes, breathe and then open them again with a new perspective and a renewed sense of control. And if that fails, a good night's sleep can change your world!

When things do feel like they're spinning out around, come back to your circles: *what is directly in your circle of control?* Only your thoughts and actions live here. *What is within your circle of influence?* What can you impact, but not control? And, finally, *what do you need to completely let go of* and accept that, no matter how hard you try or how many hours of sleep you lose, you'll never be able to change?

I'm going to leave you with one final quote. A quote that's got me through some very dark days, sleepless nights, panic attacks, breakups, debt, stress and, more regularly than I'd care to admit, the feeling of just wanting to give up. A quote that, when you live by it, I know will have as profound an impact on your life as it has on mine ...

Do what you can, with what you have, where you are.
Bill Widener (often attributed to
Theodore Roosevelt)

RESOURCES

I've referenced a lot of frameworks and models through the book. You can find them all, and supporting resources, at www.theteachershealthcoach. co.uk/healthy-habits

RECOMMENDED READING

Bethune, A. (2018) *Wellbeing in the Primary Classroom: A Practical Guide to Teaching Happiness and Positive Mental Health.* London: Bloomsbury Education.

Brown, B. (2018) *Dare to Lead: Brave Work. Tough Conversations. Whole Hearts.* London: Vermilion.

Clear, J. (2018) *Atomic Habits: An Easy and Proven Way to Build Good Habits and Break Bad Ones.* New York: Avery.

Cowley, A. (2019) *The Wellbeing Toolkit: Sustaining, Supporting and Enabling School Staff.* London: Bloomsbury Education.

Duhigg, C. (2012) *The Power of Habit: Why We Do What We Do in Life and Business.* New York: Random House.

Fogg, B.J. (2019) *Tiny Habits: The Small Changes That Change Everything.* New York: Houghton Mifflin Harcourt.

Sinek, S. (2011) *Start With Why: How Great Leaders Inspire Everyone to Take Action* London: Penguin.

Smith, J. (2022) *Why Has Nobody Told Me This Before?* London: Penguin Life.

Vignola, N. (2023) *Rewire: Break the Cycle, Alter Your Thoughts and Create Lasting Change.* London: Penguin Life.

RECOMMENDED WATCHING

Kell, E., *TEDx Talk*, Taking control and reducing the risk of burnout. www.youtube.com/watch?v=q4ZEoYM3zHw&t=614s

TOP TIPS FROM TEACHERS

The following is great advice from experienced teachers.

ON BOUNDARIES...

"Build boundaries, it's ok to say no or not yet. You are important and your mental health and wellbeing is the key. Happy mind, happy person!"

"Self-first is the most important and powerful realisation. It's not about being selfish, it's putting your needs and wants first and respecting yourself and setting the boundaries to enable others to respect that too."

"It's okay to say no and put yourself first, it doesn't make you a bad teacher or person."

"Work is simply not the be all and end all. It takes a while to come to terms with, but we aren't quite as important as we would like to think we are and when you realise - it's pretty liberating."

"You're no good to the children if you don't look after your own well-being."

"If you're an after-school chatter, then leaving work early actually helps create more time for yourself as you cut out the conversation."

ON HEALTHY HABITS...

"Nothing changes if nothing changes."

"Celebrate the small wins, as each small achievement is a step forward and brings you closer to your goals, even if it doesn't feel like it right now."

"Progress isn't always obvious in the moment but each step you take, no matter how small, is still a part of the journey you are on."

ON MENTAL HEALTH...

"Stop comparing - you are enough."

"Reach out for support if you need to or just need someone to talk to. Stopping and getting a change of environment is sometimes all you need to do."

"The power of journaling! Although it feels clunky, painful and silly at first, it's a stupidly powerful tool and can help to reshape your thoughts and feelings."

"Sometimes the setbacks and unplanned moments bring us the greatest growth. You don't have to be perfect all the time. As long as you are moving forward, even if it's not in a straight line, you are still making progress. One bad day doesn't define your week."

"By taking a step back and seeing the bigger picture you realise there is more success and resilience then you realise."

"Having watched several colleagues suffer and ultimately quit through stress, I've realised no matter how good a teacher I am, I am completely replaceable. The world will not end if you take the sick day or prioritise your rest."

ON REST...

"Rest is the most important but hardest part sometimes."

"Be strict with yourself. Tomorrow will be so much easier if you watch one less episode, don't revenge procrastinate and get an extra 30-60 mins in bed."

ON MOVEMENT AND NUTRITION...

"We need to stop seeing exercise as a luxury, something to do when you have 'time'. It's an absolute essential attribute to not only your physical, but mental health too."

"Get out for a walk at some point during the day, even if it's walking the long way round to the photocopier."

"Start small, easy and enjoyable. You'll be shocked how quickly you can become 'addicted' to the effects and just need/want more. Your body can always do more than you think too."

REFERENCES

Brown, B. (2018) *Dare to Lead: Brave Work. Tough Conversations. Whole Hearts*. London: Vermilion.

Clear, J. (2018) *Atomic Habits: An Easy and Proven Way to Build Good Habits and Break Bad Ones*. New York: Avery.

Collins, J. (2001) *Good to Great: Why Some Companies Make the Leap ... and Others Don't*. New York: HarperBusiness.

Dalton-Smith, S. Dr (n.d.) *7 Types of Rest*. www.drdaltonsmith.com/

Deckar, T. (n.d.) In the digital collection, Early English Books Online. https://name.umdl.umich.edu/A20060.0001.001. University of Michigan Library Digital Collections.

Gilbert, R. (2013) *Read This Book Tonight to Help You Win Tomorrow: Get Mentally Primed to Perform*. Scotts Valley, CA: CreateSpace Independent.

Keller, G. and Papasan, J. (2013) *The ONE Thing: The Surprisingly Simple Truth Behind Extraordinary Results*. Austin, TX: Bard Press.

Kram, O. (2021) Overcoming Burnout blog. *Her Bags Were Packed*. Available at: www.herbagswerepacked.com/blog/overcoming-burn-out

Lally, P., van Jaarsveld, C.H.M., Potts, H.W.W. and Wardle, J. (2009) How are habits formed: modelling habit formation in the real world. *European Journal of Social Psychology*, 40(6), 998–1009. https://doi.org/10.1002/ejsp.674

Layne, E. (2019) *7 Ways to Accept and Lean into a Season of Rest*. The Life on Purpose Movement. https://ericalayne.co/7-ways-to-accept-and-lean-into-a-season-of-rest/

Nagoski, E. (2019) *Burnout: The Secret to Unlocking the Stress Cycle*. London: Ballantine.

Nhat Hanh, T. (1991) *Peace Is Every Step: The Path of Mindfulness in Everyday Life*. New York: Bantam.

Smith, J. (2022) *Why Has Nobody Told Me This Before?* London: Penguin Life.

INDEX